Congressional Research Service

Informing the legislative debate since 1914 _____

The Voting Rights Act of 1965: Background and Overview

Kevin J. Coleman
Analyst in Elections

July 1, 2014

Congressional Research Service

7-5700

www.crs.gov

R43626

Summary

The Voting Rights Act (VRA) was successfully challenged in a June 2013 case decided by the U.S. Supreme Court in *Shelby County, Alabama v. Holder.* The suit challenged the constitutionality of Sections 4 and 5 of the VRA, under which certain jurisdictions with a history of racial discrimination in voting—mostly in the South—were required to "pre-clear" changes to the election process with the Justice Department (the U.S. Attorney General) or the U.S. District Court for the District of Columbia. The preclearance provision (Section 5) was based on a formula (Section 4) that considered voting practices and patterns in 1964, 1968, or 1972. At issue in *Shelby County* was whether Congress exceeded its constitutional authority when it reauthorized the VRA in 2006—with the existing formula—thereby infringing on the rights of the states. In its ruling, the Court struck down Section 4 as outdated and not "grounded in current conditions." As a consequence, Section 5 is intact, but inoperable, unless or until Congress prescribes a new Section 4 formula.

The Voting Rights Act is a landmark federal law enacted in 1965 to remove race-based restrictions on voting. It is perhaps the country's most important voting rights law, with a history that dates to the Civil War. After that conflict ended, a number of constitutional amendments were adopted that addressed the particular circumstances of freed slaves, including the Fifteenth Amendment that guaranteed the right to vote for all U.S. citizens regardless of "race, color, or previous condition of servitude."

During Reconstruction, federal troops occupied the former Confederate states as they were reintegrated into the Union. The Fifteenth Amendment achieved its purpose for a time and black voting participation and representation in the South increased rapidly. The first black representatives to Congress were elected, as well as hundreds of state and local officeholders. Reconstruction continued for a decade, until the disputed presidential election of 1876. Under the agreement known as the "Compromise of 1877" that resolved the dispute, federal troops were withdrawn from the South and the political gains of the "freedmen" were subsequently rolled back. As the Reconstruction effort receded into the past, most blacks were prevented from voting by tactics such as literacy tests, poll taxes, the grandfather clause, as well as intimidation and violence. By the turn of the 20th century, blacks were almost completely disenfranchised in the South.

The civil rights movement and the federal government made progress in regaining the franchise for black voters by mid-century, but significant impediments remained. When efforts to register voters in the Deep South in the early 1960s provoked a violent backlash, a protest march from Selma to Montgomery, Alabama was organized in March 1965. Attacks on the marchers by state troopers and others prompted the Johnson Administration to intervene and, shortly thereafter, to propose a voting rights law that called for direct federal intervention to uphold the guarantees of the Fifteenth Amendment. The Voting Rights Act was enacted on August 6, 1965, and it prohibited states from imposing qualifications or practices to deny the right to vote on account of race; permitted direct federal intervention in the electoral process in certain places, based on a "coverage formula"; and required pre-clearance of new laws in covered states' jurisdictions to ensure that they did not have the purpose, nor would have the effect, of denying the right to vote on account of race, among other provisions. Black voter registration and participation increased dramatically shortly thereafter.

This report provides background information on the historical circumstances that led to the adoption of the VRA, a summary of its major provisions, and a brief discussion of the U.S. Supreme Court decision and related legislation in the 113th Congress.

Two identical bills—H.R. 3899 and S. 1945—have been introduced that would amend the VRA by adding a new coverage formula, among other provisions. No action has occurred on either bill.

Contents

Tables

Contacts

Introduction

The voting rights of black Americans have been effectively guaranteed only since passage of the Voting Rights Act in 1965, despite a constitutional amendment adopted nearly 100 years earlier that said "[t]he right of citizens of the United States to vote shall not be denied or abridged by the United States or any State on account of race, color, or previous condition of servitude."[1] Initially, the Fifteenth Amendment profoundly changed electoral politics in the country and particularly in the former slave states. The first black Members of Congress were chosen in 1870 from Mississippi and South Carolina, respectively, and hundreds of black officeholders at all levels were elected in the following years.

By the turn of the 20th century, however, a little more than 20 years after the Reconstruction era ended, no African Americans served in Congress and all of the former Confederate states had rewritten their constitutions to exclude African Americans from voting. Despite the efforts of the National Association for the Advancement of Colored People (NAACP), founded in 1909,[2] the civil rights movement, and congressional intervention with the enactments of the Civil Rights Acts of 1957, 1960, and 1964, the status quo of black disenfranchisement remained entrenched and resistant to wholesale change until the adoption of the Voting Rights Act.[3]

Historical Overview

The political landscape of the South was completely transformed in the years after the Civil War. The Reconstruction era began with military occupation and provisional state governments in the former Confederate states until they met certain conditions to be readmitted to the union.[4] The conditions for readmission initially were based on a presidential version of Reconstruction, then according to the dictates of a series of Reconstruction acts passed when Congress took over the process. Although enfranchising the former slaves—the "freedmen"—was a matter of sharp dispute, several laws and a constitutional amendment were soon adopted to achieve that end.[5] Under the Reconstruction regime, the freedmen were enfranchised while some former Confederates were excluded from voting, temporarily establishing a new political order and completely restructuring the composition of state governments.

Presidential Reconstruction

Even before the war ended on April 9, 1865, the problem of reconciling the states once the conflict was over had been anticipated. President Lincoln's plan to "bind up the nation's

---

[1] The 15th Amendment was ratified in 1870.

[2] John Hope Franklin and Alfred A. Moss, Jr., *From Slavery to Freedom: A History of African Americans* (McGraw-Hill, Inc., 1994), p. 319.

[3] The terms "black" and "African American" are both used in this report, similar to the use of both terms in the discussion of the Voting Rights Act on the U.S Department of Justice website, which may be found here: http://www.justice.gov/crt/about/vot/intro/intro.php.

[4] Alabama, Arkansas, Florida, Louisiana, North Carolina, and South Carolina were readmitted in 1868, while Georgia, Mississippi, Texas, and Virginia were readmitted in 1870.

[5] Women were not permitted to vote in any state at the time.

wounds"[6] and reunite South and North had been outlined in a proclamation he made in December 1863. A simple oath of allegiance to support, protect, and defend the Constitution was required to obtain a full pardon, except for certain officers in the Confederate government and military, former Members of Congress who resigned to aid the rebellion, and those who had treated black persons, or the white persons responsible for them, unlawfully as prisoners of war.[7] When the number of persons who took the oath equaled one-tenth the number who had voted in the election of 1860 and a state government was reestablished, the state would be recognized and entitled to the benefits outlined in the Constitution.

In response to the plan outlined by the President in December 1863, Congress asserted its own responsibility for the political solution to reunite the country with the Wade-Davis bill, passed on July 2, 1864. The terms for readmission were less generous than those proposed by President Lincoln. The bill would have required an oath of allegiance from a majority of voters in the state before a convention to reestablish a state government in conformance with the Constitution could be held. Most of those who had participated on the Confederate side in the war would have been ineligible to vote for delegates to the convention. Lincoln pocket vetoed the measure, noting that the "free-state constitutions and governments, already adopted and installed in Arkansas and Louisiana" would be set aside under the conditions of the Wade-Davis bill, thereby discouraging further effort by loyal citizens there.[8] The disposition of the governments in Arkansas and Louisiana, as well as Tennessee, was left in doubt when Congress refused to recognize them.[9]

The Civil War ended on April 9, 1865, when General Robert E. Lee surrendered to General Ulysses S. Grant at Appomattax Court House, Virginia. President Lincoln was assassinated five days later. Although Congress had already passed the Thirteenth Amendment that abolished slavery, it had not yet been ratified. Lincoln believed the Amendment to be crucial to the Reconstruction effort by making permanent the decree set forth in the Emancipation Proclamation. How he would have proceeded with respect to the important question of suffrage for the freedmen is not known.

Lincoln's Vice President, Andrew Johnson, upon succeeding to the presidency, pursued a plan that soon alienated many in Congress who believed Reconstruction was a congressional prerogative and distrusted his motives in any case. President Johnson issued two proclamations in May 1865, before the 39th Congress had convened, concerning both his overall Reconstruction policy and a specific plan for North Carolina, due to the lack of a Union military government in the state. The first proclamation required an oath of loyalty from former Confederates to receive a pardon, excluding certain officials who had served in the Confederacy, as well as those who owned over $20,000 in taxable property, a provision aimed at large landowners. The North Carolina plan called for appointing a provisional governor who would hold an election for delegates to a state constitutional convention, with eligible voters defined as those who were eligible to vote on the day the state seceded from the Union, excluding the freedmen as a result.

---

[6] "Second Inaugural Address, March 4, 1865," in *The Collected Works of Abraham Lincoln*, ed. Roy P. Basler, Marion Dolores Pratt, and Lloyd A. Dunlap, vol. VII (New Brunswick, New Jersey: Rutgers University Press, 1953), pp.332-333.

[7] "Proclamation of Amnesty and Reconstruction, December 8, 1863," in *The Collected Works of Abraham Lincoln*, Basler, Pratt, and Dunlap, vol. VII, pp. 53-56.

[8] "Proclamation Concerning Reconstruction, July 8, 1864," in *The Collected Works of Abraham Lincoln*, Basler, Pratt, and Dunlap, vol. VII, pp. 433-434.

[9] Military governments had been established in these states when the Union Army took control of the states in the early years of the war.

The plan would serve as the model for admitting the other six states in which no military government existed. With respect to black suffrage in the reorganized states, the Administration left the determination to each state convention.[10] None of the provisional governments extended the vote to the freedmen.

In the following months, President Johnson communicated his preferred terms informally to provisional governors, although he did not insist on ratification of the Thirteenth Amendment or enfranchisement of the freedmen. Once the provisional state governments were established, the election of representatives at the state and federal level resumed. In response to the President's reluctance to dictate terms to the former Confederate states, newly elected legislatures enacted "black codes" to control the behavior of the freedmen, including laws that limited property ownership; banned ownership of firearms; limited jury service and court testimony; and imposed penalties of imprisonment or fines for vagrancy, violating work contracts, and violating curfews.[11] Elections for the U.S. Congress signaled further obstinacy, when those elected included the former vice president of the Confederacy, as well as numerous former Confederate army officers and members of the Confederate Congress.[12] These actions were not well received in Washington. Congress refused to seat any of the elected representatives from former Confederate states[13] and eventually moved to take control of the Reconstruction process from the President.

By year's end, the requisite number of states had ratified the Thirteenth Amendment—the first of the "Civil War Amendments."

Congressional Reconstruction

In early 1866, President Johnson's veto of bills to extend the Freedman's Bureau (that assisted former slaves) and to establish the freedmen's civil rights under law, aimed in part at the black codes, dispelled entirely any notion of cooperation with Congress on Reconstruction. Congress overrode the veto of the civil rights bill and established a joint committee on Reconstruction for all related matters. Congress also passed a constitutional amendment that largely addressed the circumstances of the freedmen (but which also applied to the entire nation). The Fourteenth Amendment—the second of the Civil War Amendments—defined citizenship, provided for equal protection under the laws, and reduced representation in Congress for any state that denied the vote to male citizens 21 years of age.[14] Given the high tensions surrounding the Reconstruction effort, it was a relatively moderate measure overall and, while it reduced representation for counting freedmen without extending the franchise to them, it did not mandate black male suffrage. The amendment was submitted to the states for ratification in June, 1866.

---

[10] Brooks D. Simpson, *The Reconstruction Presidents* (Lawrence, KS: University Press of Kansas, 1998), pp. 74-75.

[11] Ibid., p. 82.

[12] Franklin and Moss, *From Slavery to Freedom*, p. 225.

[13] Brooks D. Simpson, *The Reconstruction Presidents,* p. 92.

[14] The Fourteenth Amendment, ratified by the requisite number of states in 1868, guarantees state and federal citizenship to all persons born or naturalized in the U.S.; prohibits states from abridging citizens' rights or depriving them of life, liberty, or property without due process of law; requires states to provide equal protection under the law to all citizens; set out the means for reducing a state's representation in Congress if the vote is denied to eligible individuals; prohibits office-holding by former state and federal elected officials who took an oath to support the Constitution of the U.S. but engaged in insurrection or rebellion against it or gave aid and comfort to those who did; asserts the validity of the public debt for the war; and gives Congress the power to enforce the Amendment.

Congress also passed a series of four Reconstruction acts in 1867 and 1868 for the purpose of reintegrating southern states. The first Reconstruction Act of 1867, enacted on March 2, noted that "no legal State governments or adequate protection for life or property now exists in the former rebel States of Virginia, North Carolina, South Carolina, Georgia, Mississippi, Alabama, Louisiana, Florida, Texas, and Arkansas; and ... it is necessary that peace and good order should be enforced in said States until loyal and republican State governments can be legally established."[15]

In forming new state governments under the act, the South was divided into five military districts under the authority of an army officer with "sufficient military force to enable such officer to perform his duties and enforce his authority."[16] States were called on to hold a convention to adopt a new constitution that conformed to the U.S. Constitution; extend voting rights to black males and include protections in the state constitution; submit the constitution for approval by voters; and approve the proposed Fourteenth Amendment in the legislature elected under the new constitution. Some former Confederates were excluded from voting.

The Second Reconstruction Act, enacted on March 23, 1867,[17] described the process of holding the state convention and approving a new constitution. It called for the commanding generals in each district to register eligible voters and prescribed a stringent oath of allegiance to be taken by each voter. In the election, voters would elect delegates to the state convention and would also vote on whether a convention should be held. If a majority approved the convention, it was subsequently convened to draft a new constitution, which was then submitted for approval by a majority of voters. Once the constitution was submitted to and approved by Congress, the state was entitled to resume electing federal representatives. In the meantime, 703,000 freedmen and 627,000 whites registered to vote.[18]

The battle between the President and Congress continued when the execution of the Reconstruction Acts provided the opportunity for Johnson to meddle in the details.[19] In response to certain ambiguities that arose about the processes described therein, the Attorney General issued opinions on how the laws should be interpreted. Shortly thereafter, Congress passed the Third and Fourth Reconstruction Acts to clarify its intent. The Third Reconstruction Act, passed on July 19, 1867,[20] asserted the authority of the military commanders in the affected states and clarified the role and responsibilities of the boards of registration. The Fourth Reconstruction Act, passed on March 9, 1868,[21] concerned the details of elections to accept or reject the new state constitutions and defined who was eligible to vote in such elections. The act stipulated that proposed constitutions could be approved by a majority of voters, rather than a majority of those registered, thereby preventing efforts by some to disrupt the process by boycotting it. By the

---

[15] 14 Stat. 428.

[16] Ibid.

[17] 15 Stat. 2-5.

[18] Francis L. Broderick, *Reconstruction and the American Negro, 1865-1900* (London: The Macmillan Company, 1969), p. 45.

[19] The conflict between Congress and the President over Reconstruction and related matters led to Johnson's impeachment; his trial in the Senate concluded when votes on the articles of impeachment that would have removed him from office failed by one vote margins, 35-19. Brooks D. Simpson, *The Reconstruction Presidents,* pp. 126-127.

[20] 15 Stat. 14-16.

[21] 15 Stat. 40-41.

summer of 1868, Alabama, Arkansas, Florida, Georgia, Louisiana, South Carolina, and North Carolina had approved constitutions and been readmitted as states.

At the federal level, the Fifteenth Amendment—the last of the Civil War Amendments—was ratified in 1870. It guarantees the right to vote for all U.S. citizens regardless of "race, color, or previous condition of servitude." With this amendment in place and a Republican Congress in charge of Reconstruction and committed to improving the condition of the freedmen, the level of black electoral participation and representation increased dramatically.[22] The remaining former Confederate states of Mississippi, Texas, and Virginia were readmitted in 1870, after submitting to additional conditions that included ratification of the Fifteenth Amendment.

Election of Black Members of Congress from the South

The first black Members of Congress took their seats in 1870, when Hiram Rhodes Revels was elected by the Mississippi state senate to fill a vacant U.S. Senate seat and Joseph H. Rainey was elected to fill a vacant U.S. House of Representatives seat in the South Carolina delegation (see **Table 1** below).[23] In the years that followed, black officials were elected at all levels of government and the newfound political influence was evident in appointed federal offices as well, as blacks took office as ambassadors, Census officials, customs appointments, U.S. marshalls and Treasury agents, and mail agents and Post Office officials.[24]

In many of the former Confederate states, hundreds of black officeholders were elected in the Reconstruction period, including Alabama (167), Georgia (108), Louisiana (210), Mississippi (226), North Carolina (180), and South Carolina (316).[25] The electoral gains were remarkable, having occurred in states where the freedman had been enslaved only years earlier and provided testimony to the determination of Reconstruction Congresses, as well as the presence of federal troops.

Table 1. African American Members of the U.S. Congress, 1870-1901

Name	Party Affiliation and State	Years of Service
U.S. Senate		
Hiram R. Revels	R-Mississippi	1870-71
Blanche K. Bruce	R-Mississippi	1875-81
U.S. House of Representatives		
Joseph H. Rainey	R-South Carolina	1870-79
Jefferson F. Long	R-Georgia	1870-71

---

[22] At the time of the Civil War, five states in the North granted full suffrage to blacks: Maine, Massachusetts, New Hampshire, New York, Rhode Island, and Vermont. Kirk Harold Porter, *A History of Suffrage in the United States* (New York: AMS Press, 1918), p. 90.

[23] CRS Report RL30378, *African American Members of the United States Congress: 1870-2012*, by Jennifer E. Manning and Colleen J. Shogan, p. 4.

[24] Eric Foner, *Freedom's Lawmakers: A Directory of Black Officeholders during Reconstruction* (Baton Rouge: Louisiana State University Press, 1996), p. xv.

[25] Ibid, p. xiv.

Name	Party Affiliation and State	Years of Service
Robert B. Elliot	R-South Carolina	1871-74
Robert C. DeLarge	R-South Carolina	1871-73
Benjamin S. Turner	R-Alabama	1871-73
Josiah T. Walls	R-Florida	1871-73
Richard H. Caine	R-South Carolina	1873-75 1877-79
John R. Lynch	R-Mississippi	1873-77 1882-83
James T. Rapier	R-Alabama	1873-75
Alonzo J. Ransier	R- South Carolina	1873-75
Jeremiah Haralson	R- Alabama	1875-77
John A. Hyman	R-North Carolina	1875-77
Charles E. Nash	R-Louisiana	1875-77
Robert Smalls	R-South Carolina	1875-79
James E. O-Hara	R-North Carolina	1883-87
Henry P. Cheatham	R-North Carolina	1889-93
John M. Langston	R-Virginia	1890-91
Thomas E. Miller	R-South Carolina	1890-91
George W. Murray	R-South Carolina	1893-95 1896-97
George W. White	R-North Carolina	1897-1901

Source: CRS Report RL30378, *African American Members of the United States Congress: 1870-2012*, by Jennifer E. Manning and Colleen J. Shogan.

The End of Reconstruction and the "Jim Crow" South

The transition to black political participation did not go unchallenged or unexploited, however. Blacks, Republicans, and sometimes poor whites were the target of intimidation and violence across the South, particularly during the election season. The Ku Klux Klan was founded in 1866 in Tennessee and soon unleashed across the South a "reign of terror" against "Republican leaders black and white" that included assassinations of political leaders, such as Congressman James M. Hinds and three members of the South Carolina legislature.[26] The Klan was not the only violent secret society:

> For ten years after 1867 there flourished the Knights of the White Camelia, the Constitutional Union Guards, the Pale Faces, the White Brotherhood, the Council of Safety, the '76 Association.... the White League of Louisiana, The White Line of Mississippi, and the Rifle Clubs of South Carolina. White Southerners expected to do by extralegal or

---

[26] Eric Foner, *Reconstruction: America's Unfinished Revolution, 1863-1877* (New York: Harper & Row, Publishers, 1988), p. 342.

blatantly illegal means what had not been allowed by law: to exercise absolute control over blacks, drive them and their fellows from power, and establish "white supremacy."[27]

In one Louisiana Parish, a mob destroyed the Republican newspaper and drove the editor out of town before turning on the local black population and killing 200. A local sheriff in Camilla, Georgia led an armed group of 400 whites to attack a black election parade and then track down and kill many who had fled to the countryside.[28] In Louisiana alone in the Presidential election year of 1868, an estimated 1,081 persons, most of them black, were killed by state Democrats.[29] The number of blacks killed in southern cities was likewise shocking: 46 in Memphis and 34 in New Orleans in 1866, 25-30 in Meridian, Mississippi and 34 in Vicksburg in 1875, and 105 in Colfax, Louisiana on Easter Sunday, 1873.[30] State officials were unwilling or unable to stop the violence.

Reconstruction policies were not sustained due to other factors as well. Corruption plagued Republican governments in the South and the presence of "scalawags" (native Southerners who cooperated in the Reconstruction effort out of self-interest or on principle) and "carpetbaggers" (Northerners who came south to exploit or support the Reconstruction program) provoked further resentment. At the same time, the number of white Southerners who had taken the oath of allegiance or otherwise received amnesty grew. When the oath was repealed in 1871, nearly all ex-Confederates were again entitled to vote. Meanwhile, Democrats regained control of governments in North Carolina and Virginia in 1870, followed by Texas, Arkansas, and Alabama by 1875. As the Presidential election of 1876 approached, Republicans controlled only Louisiana, Florida, and South Carolina. Finally, a number of well-known champions of Reconstruction in Congress had died and general sentiment in the North regarding the effort was one of fatigue. As conservative Democrats reasserted themselves in the South, these factors, in combination with threatened and actual violence, doomed the effort to permanently enfranchise the freedmen.

"Compromise of 1877" Formally Ends Reconstruction

Reconstruction came to a formal end with the "Compromise of 1877" that resolved the deadlocked 1876 election. Democrat Samuel L. Tilden was initially thought to have won, although his Electoral College vote total of 184 was one less than the 185 needed for election. Voting in the South was marred by fraud, intimidation, and other illegal practices on both sides and the resolution of the contest came down to contested electoral votes in Florida, South Carolina, and Louisiana. Congress deadlocked on which sets of electoral votes to count and an electoral commission was established to resolve the dispute. The commission awarded all three sets of electoral votes to Hayes on a party-line vote. Faced with possible violence and controversy over the legitimacy of the Hayes presidency, Republican operatives and southern Democrats negotiated an unwritten, informal agreement that became known as the "Compromise of 1877."[31]

Under the agreement, the government removed from the South all federal troops, which had provided at least limited protection to blacks who went to the polls to vote. The latter part of the

---

[27] Franklin and Moss, *From Slavery to Freedom,* p. 249.

[28] Foner, *Reconstruction*, p. 342.

[29] J. Morgan Kousser, *Colorblind Justice: Minority Voting Rights and the Undoing of the Second Reconstruction,* (Chapel Hill, The University of North Carolina Press, 1999), p. 23.

[30] Ibid.

[31] Foner, *Reconstruction,* pp. 575-582.

19th century was marked by a reversal in political dominance as Reconstruction ended and Democrats imposed racial boundaries to subvert the civil rights laws and Civil War amendments that had briefly transformed the region.

As the disenfranchisement effort gained momentum, a number of states called constitutional conventions for the express purpose of enacting the means to prevent blacks from voting. Disenfranchisement schemes included poll taxes, literacy tests, and grandfather and old soldier clauses (see **Table 2** below). Mississippi led the way with a constitutional convention in 1890 which "served more or less as a model for other states seeking to circumvent the war amendments and legally disfranchise the negro."[32] The state's population at the time included 743,000 blacks and 545,000 whites.[33] The convention adopted a poll tax of $2 for every citizen between the ages of 21 and 60, with the requirement that the tax receipt be presented in order to vote,[34] a detail that could be easily forgotten or enforced on a selective basis to exclude individual voters. Also adopted was a provision that excluded those convicted of various crimes, as well as a literacy test that might require satisfactorily reading, understanding, or interpreting any section of the state constitution.[35]

Other states quickly followed Mississippi's example. South Carolina held a constitutional convention in 1895 led by former governor and then U.S. Senator "Pitchfork Ben" Tillman, nationally known white supremacist and proponent of forced black disenfranchisement.[36] The convention adopted a two-year residence requirement; a $1 poll tax; a literacy test that required reading, writing, or understanding any section of the state constitution,[37] or ownership of property worth $300; and the disqualification of convicts. Louisiana added the "grandfather clause" to the list of disenfranchising tactics when its constitution was amended in 1898. The provision directed that the registration list include the names of all males whose fathers and grandfathers were registered on January 1, 1867, before blacks had been enfranchised. The state also imposed educational and property requirements for voting, from which those who qualified under the grandfather clause were exempt.[38] Similarly, the old soldier clause exempted veterans of the Civil War and other specified wars from having to submit to a literacy test.[39] Rates of illiteracy for adult black males were significant in some states: 55% in South Carolina and 53% in North Carolina in 1900,[40] for example, both of which had enacted reading and writing literacy requirements by that time.[41]

---

[32] Kirk Harold Porter, *A History of Suffrage in the United States* (New York: AMS Press, 1971), pp. 208-209.

[33] U.S. Department of Commerce, Bureau of the Census, *Historical Statistics of the United States, Colonial Times to 1970, Bicentennial Edition* (Washington, DC: Government Printing Office, 1975), p. 30. Other states with a majority black population in 1890 included Louisiana and South Carolina. In addition, Alabama had a black population of 45% and Georgia had a black population of 47%.

[34] Ibid.

[35] John Hope Franklin and Alfred A. Moss, Jr., *From Slavery to Freedom: A History of African Americans*, 7th ed. (McGraw-Hill, Inc., 1994), p. 259.

[36] *Dictionary of American Biography*, Dumas Malone ed. (New York: Charles Scribner's Sons, 1936), pp. 547-549. The nickname "Pitchfork Ben" resulted from his exhortation to voters that, if they sent him to Washington, he would stick his pitchfork into President Cleveland's ribs. He had been a farmer before entering politics.

[37] Non-southern states that had a literacy test for voting in 1900 included California, Connecticut, Delaware, Maine, Massachusetts, Washington, and Wyoming; Jerrold G. Rusk, *A Statistical History of the American Electorate* (Washington, DC: CQ Press, 2001), p. 35.

[38] Franklin, *From Slavery to Freedom: A History of African Americans*, p. 260.

[39] Porter, *A History of Suffrage in the United States*, p. 35.

[40] J. Morgan Kousser, *The Shaping of Southern Politics: Suffrage Restriction and the Establishment of the One-Party* (continued...)

Table 2. Poll Taxes, Grandfather Clauses, Old Soldier Clauses, and Literacy Tests Enacted in Former Confederate States, 1890-1918

State	Poll Tax	Grandfather Clause	Old Soldier Clause	Literacy Test
Alabama	X	X	X	X
Arkansas	X[a]			
Florida	X			
Georgia	X[b]	X	X	X
Louisiana	X	X	X	X
Mississippi	X			X
North Carolina	X	X		X
South Carolina	X			X
Tennessee	X			
Texas	X			
Virginia	X[c]	X	X	X

Source: Jerrold G. Rusk, *A Statistical History of the American Electorate* (Washington, DC: CQ Press, 2001), pp. 33-35.

Notes:

a. The poll tax amendment was declared enforceable by the Speaker of the Arkansas House of Representatives in 1893, but was declared invalid by a U.S. Circuit Court on a technicality in 1905. The legislature approved a new poll tax amendment in 1907 which was passed by voters in 1908.

b. Georgia enacted a poll tax in 1801 that applied to property-less white males. It was applied to all males in 1877 and modified in 1908 to require that all poll taxes and other taxes owed since adoption of the 1877 state constitution must be paid to be eligible to vote.

c. Virginia enacted a poll tax in 1876 that was repealed in 1882. It was re-enacted in 1902 along with a literacy test. A grandfather clause and an old soldier clause were enacted in 1902 and provided alternatives to the literacy test. After 1904, the old soldier clause provided an exception to the poll tax.

Disenfranchising conventions followed in Alabama, Georgia, North Carolina, and Virginia, and the border state of Oklahoma. In addition to the legal measures adopted to eliminate the black vote, the intimidation and violence that had been directed at blacks during Reconstruction rose in the years after 1877 and continued into the 20th century, particularly in the form of lynching. Between 1884 and 1900, 2,500 lynchings were reported nationwide and most victims were black. While the barbarism occurred in both North and South, the largest numbers of lynchings occurred in Alabama, Georgia, Mississippi, and Louisiana.[42] In the South, the bloodshed was inextricably linked to maintaining white supremacy.

The effect of these disenfranchising measures and the related violence was immediate: in Alabama, for example, of the 181,471 black males of voting age in 1900, 3,000 were registered.

(...continued)

South, 1880-1910 (New Haven and London: Yale University Press, 1974), p. 50.

[41] Rusk, *A Statistical History of the American Electorate*, p. 34.

[42] Franklin, *From Slavery to Freedom: A History of African Americans,* p. 312.

In Louisiana in 1896, there were 130,344 blacks registered to vote; by 1900, the number had dropped to 5,320.[43]

"Jim Crow" Laws

In addition to driving blacks out of the political arena, southern legislatures enacted measures to require the separation of whites and blacks in general society. The "Jim Crow" laws of the late 19th century segregated the races with respect to public places and accommodations, including on trains and in hotels, restaurants, barber shops, and theatres. The U.S. Supreme Court upheld the constitutionality of state-mandated segregation in public facilities on a 7-1 vote in *Plessy v. Ferguson* in 1896.[44] The majority opinion stated, in part,

> We consider the underlying fallacy of the plaintiff's argument to consist in the assumption that the enforced separation of the two races stamps the colored race with a badge of inferiority. If this be so, it is not by reason of anything found in the act, but solely because the colored race chooses to put that construction upon it …The argument also assumes that social prejudices may be overcome by legislation, and that equal rights cannot be secured to the negro except by an enforced commingling of the two races. We cannot accept this proposition. If the two races are to meet upon terms of social equality, it must be the result of natural affinities, a mutual appreciation of each other's merits, and a voluntary consent of individuals.

By the turn of the 20th century, black registration[45] and voting[46] in the South had been greatly reduced, despite the guarantees of the Fifteenth Amendment, and the social circumstances of black citizens were severely restricted under a regional network of Jim Crow laws and an underlying culture of intimidation and outright violence, despite the proclamations of the Fourteenth Amendment. Decades would pass before the segregated and unequal racial dynamic of the South was successfully challenged. Even as the country was fighting fascism abroad in 1944, fewer than "5 percent of the adult Negro population [,] had voted in the southern states within the previous five years" according to sociologist and economist Gunnar Myrdal.[47]

Passing the Voting Rights Act in 1965

The effort to regain black voting rights advanced slowly in the new century. The National Association for the Advancement of Colored People (NAACP) and the American Civil Liberties Union (ACLU) secured important legal victories when the grandfather clause was struck down by the U.S. Supreme Court in 1915,[48] followed by the "white primary" in 1944.[49] The white primary

---

[43] Ibid, p. 261.

[44] 163 U.S. 537.

[45] Black registration was reduced to single digits in most southern states after disenfranchising laws were enacted, according to estimates: 1.3% in Alabama in 1902, 4.3% in Georgia in 1910, 1.1% in Louisiana in 1904, 7.1% in Mississippi in 1904, 4.6% in North Carolina in 1904, between 3.8% and 13.8% in South Carolina between 1896 and 1904, and 15.2% in Virginia in 1904. Kousser, *Shaping of Southern Politics*, p. 61.

[46] According to one account, "While the NAACP was pursuing its cause through the judiciary, Negroes barely maintained a tradition of voting in the South, and this use of the franchise was confined mostly to urban areas." Steven F. Lawson, *Black Ballots: Voting Rights in the South, 1944-1969* (Lanham, MD: Lexington Books, 1999), 19.

[47] Ibid, p. 22.

[48] Guinn and Beal v. United States, 238 U.S. 347 (1915).

had been adopted after the grandfather clause was ruled unconstitutional; it barred blacks from participating in Democratic primary elections where officeholders at all levels were effectively elected, due to the eventual decline of the Republican Party following Reconstruction. On the domestic front, thousands of black veterans returned to the United States in the years after World War II, after fighting for freedom and democracy abroad. By mid-century, the civil rights movement was gaining momentum and drawing greater attention to racial inequalities nationwide, and particularly in the South.

One event that spurred action on voting rights legislation was the Selma to Montgomery, Alabama civil rights march that took place over several weeks in March 1965.[50] A coalition of civil rights groups, led by the Student Nonviolent Coordinating Committee (SNCC), had targeted the states of the Deep South for voter registration efforts in previous years, which met with widespread, violent resistance. Three civil rights workers involved in the campaign were murdered in Neshoba County, Mississippi in 1964, in addition to 80 beatings and 65 bombings of homes, churches, and other buildings.[51] The 54-mile march was intended to draw attention to the violent resistance to black voter registration efforts that had, after several years, added only 335 new voters (of 30,000 eligible) in Dallas County, where Selma is located.[52] On March 7, marchers were attacked and turned back by state troopers and local lawmen with clubs, whips, and tear gas at Edmund Pettus Bridge as they were leaving Selma. Two days later, Martin Luther King, Jr. led a second march that turned back at a police barricade at the bridge. The march was eventually completed after President Lyndon Johnson federalized the Alabama National Guard to protect the marchers, whose numbers had swelled to approximately 25,000 by the time they reached Montgomery.[53]

In a televised address to a joint session of Congress concerning the violence in Selma and the denial of voting rights, President Johnson said,

> At times, history and fate meet at a single time in single place to shape a turning point in man's unending search for freedom. So it was at Lexington and Concord. So it was a century ago at Appomattox. So it was last week in Selma, Ala.... There is no cause for pride in what has happened in Selma. There is no cause for self-satisfaction in the long denial of equal rights of millions of Americans. But there is cause for hope and for faith in our democracy in what is happening here tonight.... Wednesday, I will send to Congress a law designed to eliminate illegal barriers to the right to vote.... This bill will strike down restrictions to voting in all elections, Federal, state and local, which have been used to deny Negroes the right to vote.[54]

(...continued)

[49] Smith v. Allwright, 321 U.S. 649 (1944).

[50] Chandler Davidson, "The Voting Rights Act: A Brief History," in *Controversies in Minority Voting: The Voting Rights Act in Perspective*, ed. Bernard Grofman and Chandler Davidson (Washington, DC: The Brookings Institution, 1992), pp. 14-17.

[51] David J. Garrow, *Protest at Selma: Martin Luther King, Jr., and the Voting Rights Act of 1965* (New Haven and London: Yale University Press, 1978), p. 21.

[52] Grofman and Davidson, *Controversies in Minority Voting*, p. 15.

[53] David J. Garrow, *Protest at Selma*, p. 117.

[54] "Transcript of the Johnson Address on Voting Rights to Joint Session of Congress," *The New York Times*, March 16, 1965, p. 30.

In contrast to earlier laws that relied on legal options to challenge southern intransigence, the bill called for direct, federal intervention to register eligible voters and imposed criminal penalties for voter interference. The Civil Rights Acts of 1957,[55] 1960,[56] and 1964[57] had included provisions intended to guarantee voting rights but, according to the Johnson Administration Attorney General Nicholas Katzenbach, "had only minimal effect. They [were] too slow."[58] The proposed "Voting Rights Act of 1965" abandoned that measured approach and called for certain states and jurisdictions to demonstrate progress, while submitting to federal oversight of voting changes. It was intended "[t]o enforce the fifteenth amendment to the Constitution of the United States, and for other purposes."

The administration proposal was introduced in the House (H.R. 6400) on March 17, 1965—two days after the President's address—and in the Senate (S. 1564) on March 18. After several months of debate and deliberation, the bill passed the House on August 3 and the Senate on August 4. The roll call vote in the House was 328-74 to adopt the conference report on S. 1564 (H. Rept. 711), and the roll call vote in the Senate was 79-18. President Johnson signed the VRA into law on August 6, 1965.[59]

The impact of the VRA was immediate and dramatic (see **Table 3** below). Nearly a million black voters were registered within four years of passage,[60] including over 50% of the black voting age population in every southern state.[61] Furthermore, the number of black elected officials in the South more than doubled, from 72 to 159, after the 1966 elections.[62]

In the years since the VRA was enacted, the U.S. Department of Justice has pursued actions against numerous states and jurisdictions in enforcing the law.[63] The Department has also reviewed more than half a million voting changes submitted under Section 5.[64]

Table 3. Percentage of Voting Age African Americans Registered to Vote in Southern States, 1947-66

State	1947	1952	1956	1966
Alabama	1.2%	5%	11%	51.2%
Arkansas	17.3%	27%	36%	59.7%
Florida	15.4%	33%	32%	60.9%
Georgia	18.8%	23%	27%	47.2%

---

[55] P.L. 85-315.

[56] P.L. 86-449.

[57] P.L. 88-352.

[58] Garrow, *Protest at Selma*, p. 113.

[59] P.L.89-110.

[60] *Guide to U.S. Elections*, 6th ed., vol. 1 (Washington, DC: CQ Press, 2010), p. 33.

[61] United States Commission on Civil Rights, *Political Participation: A Report of the United States Commission on Civil Rights* (Washington, DC: U.S. Government Printing Office, 1968), p. 13.

[62] David J. Garrow, *Protest at Selma*, p. 190.

[63] A partial list of cases may be found here: http://www.justice.gov/crt/about/vot/litigation/caselist.php.

[64] A table of changes submitted for preclearance since 1965 may be found here: http://www.justice.gov/crt/about/vot/sec_5/changes.php.

State	1947	1952	1956	1966
Louisiana	2.6%	25%	31%	47.1%
Mississippi	0.9%	4%	5%	32.9%
North Carolina	15.2%	18%	24%	51%
South Carolina	13%	20%	27%	51.4%
Tennessee	25.8%	25%	27%	71.7%
Texas	18.5%	31%	37%	61.6%
Virginia	13.2%	16%	19%	46.9%

Source: Hanes Walton, Jr., *Black Politics: A Theoretical and Structural Analysis* (New York: J.B. Lippincott Company, 1972), p. 44.

Major Provisions of the Voting Rights Act of 1965, Including Provision Ruled Unconstitutional by the U.S. Supreme Court in June 2013

The Voting Rights Act has been amended five times since it was signed into law in 1965. Below are the major provisions of the Voting Rights Act as enacted in 1965, including Section 4, the provision that was struck down by the U.S. Supreme Court in June 2013.[65]

The original law was scheduled to expire five years after it was enacted, but it has been extended and amended five times, most recently for 25 years in 2006. Brief summaries of the amendments of 1970, 1975, 1982, 1992, and 2006 follow after the discussion of the major provisions of the original law, which included the following:

- prohibited states and political subdivisions from imposing or applying qualifications, standards, practices or procedures to deny or abridge the right to vote on account or race or color (Sec. 2, *discussed in greater detail below*);

- established a coverage formula under which federal intervention in the electoral process was permitted in states and political subdivisions in which any test or device was used as a condition of voter registration on November 1, 1964 election and either less than 50% of persons of voting age were registered on that date or less than 50% of persons of voting age voted in the election of November 1964 election (Sec. 4(b), *discussed in greater detail below*);

- authorized the appointment of federal voting examiners (Sec. 3, *discussed in greater detail below*) by the Civil Service Commission (Sec. 6) to determine the qualifications, and require the enrollment, of individuals by state and local officials to vote in all federal, state, and local elections (Sec. 7);

- suspended the use of literacy tests in covered jurisdictions (Sec. 4);

---

[65] Shelby County, Alabama v. Holder, 133 S. Ct. 2612 (2013).

- required that new voting laws in covered states and local jurisdictions be approved, before taking effect, by the Attorney General or federal court, on the basis of a determination that the law did not have the purpose, nor would have the effect, of denying or abridging the right to vote on account of race or color (Sec. 5, *discussed in greater detail below*);

- included a Congressional finding that the poll tax precluded persons of limited means from voting, or imposed an unreasonable financial hardship on them as a precondition for voting, did not serve a legitimate state purpose in the conduct of elections and, in some places, had the purpose or effect of denying or abridging the right to vote on the basis of race or color; thus, Congress declared that the constitutional right to vote is denied or abridged in some places by the imposition of a poll tax (Sec. 10);

- prohibited any person, acting under color of law or otherwise, from intimidating, threatening, or coercing any person for attempting to vote or voting (Sec. 11);

Among the most significant of these provisions were the coverage formula and the requirement in covered states and jurisdictions to submit voting changes for "preclearance" before they could take effect. Until the recent U.S. Supreme Court decision that struck down Section 4, the two provisions worked together to prevent the enactment of *new* discriminatory voting laws, while other provisions focused on the status quo at the time by reiterating the intent of the Fifteenth Amendment to guarantee the right to vote without regard to race or color and banning practices to suppress voting, such as the use of literacy tests, poll taxes, and other similar devices, as well as intimidation and threats. Selected provisions of the VRA of 1965 are discussed in more detail below.

Prohibition of Practices to Deny the Right to Vote Based on Race (Sec. 2)

Section 2 applies nationwide and prohibits states and political subdivisions from imposing election practices and procedures designed to deny the right to vote based on race or color (later expanded to include language minority groups). Practices that might be adapted to have a discriminatory effect include redistricting plans, at-large elections (thereby diluting minority voting strength in the jurisdiction),[66] and voter registration procedures. The section prohibits election practices and procedures that are intended to be racially discriminatory, as well as those that have a discriminatory impact (under the 1982 amendments), and allows for the Attorney General or private citizens to initiate a lawsuit challenging a practice or procedure.

A number of important court cases have shaped the legal interpretation of Section 2, many of which have concerned challenges to at-large elections. In an important 1980 case, *Mobile v. Bolden,*[67] black residents of Mobile, Alabama, filed a class-action suit that challenged the at-large election scheme to elect the city's three commissioners. No black commissioner had ever been elected and blacks constituted about 35% of the population. The U.S. Supreme Court rejected the plaintiffs' claim and found that it was necessary to prove discriminatory intent with respect to the

---

[66] For an overview of redistricting and a discussion of vote dilution, see CRS Report R42831, *Congressional Redistricting: An Overview*, by Royce Crocker; for a discussion of redistricting and pertinent case law, see CRS Report R42482, *Congressional Redistricting and the Voting Rights Act: A Legal Overview*, by L. Paige Whitaker.

[67] 446 U.S. 55 (1980).

Mobile election scheme. The disproportionate effect of at-large elections was not sufficient to establish unconstitutional racial vote dilution.

Several years later, the Court set out a three-pronged test for proving minority vote dilution under Section 2 in *Thornburg v. Gingles*.[68] The elements included a demonstration that the minority group is (1) sufficiently large and geographically compact to be the majority in a single member district, (2) politically cohesive, and (3) the white majority votes as a bloc so that the minority's preferred candidate is usually defeated. The Court also noted that a violation may be established by considering the "totality of circumstances" and because plaintiffs "do not have an equal opportunity to participate in the political process" and elect candidates of their choice. Finally, in *Bartlett v. Strickland* in 2009, the Court held that a minority group must constitute more than 50% with respect to the geographic compactness established in the first prong of the test in *Thornburg*. The ruling determined that the ability of the minority group to elect the preferred candidate—without constituting a majority of the voting age population, but by joining with other voters—did not meet the test.

Unlike other sections of the VRA, Section 2 does not have an expiration date.

The "Bail-in" Provision (Sec. 3)[69]

The law authorizes a federal court to require the appointment of federal examiners to ensure voting rights in a jurisdiction whenever the Attorney General or an aggrieved person has brought suit to enforce the guarantees of the Fourteenth and Fifteenth Amendments. The provision applies nationwide. The examiners are appointed by the U.S. Civil Service Commission to serve, as determined by the court, in places and for a period of time appropriate to enforce the guarantees of the Fourteenth and Fifteenth Amendments. The court is also authorized to retain jurisdiction in a state or political subdivision when it has found violations of the Fifteenth Amendment (similar to the preclearance requirement in Section 5), based on a proceeding instituted by the Attorney General, during which time no changes to voting qualifications or prerequisites may be made without a determination from the court that the "qualification, prerequisite, standard, practice, or procedure does not have the purpose and will not have the effect of denying or abridging the right to vote on account of race or color." However, such changes may be enforced by the state if submitted by the chief legal officer or another appropriate official to the Attorney General, who has not interposed an objection within 60 days of submission. A later action to enjoin enforcement can still be pursued.

Following the June 2013 U.S. Supreme Court decision that struck down Section 4 (b) of the VRA, the Attorney General announced that the Justice Department would challenge changes to voting laws in Texas under Section 3. In a speech before the National Urban League annual conference on July 25, 2013, the Attorney General said the Department would "ask a federal court in Texas to subject the State of Texas to a preclearance regime similar to the one required by Section 5 of the Voting Rights Act" and would continue such efforts in the future "to fully utilize

---

[68] 478 U.S. 30 (1986).

[69] For a more detailed discussion of Section 3, see CRS Legal Sidebar, What is the "Bail In" Provision of the Voting Rights Act?, by L. Paige Whitaker

the law's remaining sections to ensure that the voting rights of all American citizens are protected."[70]

The Coverage Formula (Sec. 4)[71] [72]

The law provided for federal intervention in the electoral process—traditionally a matter for the states—in places where there was evidence that voting discrimination had occurred. It was assumed that low registration and voting statistics in jurisdictions that required literacy tests and devices resulted from their discriminatory application. Consequently, according to the formula established in Section 4(b), states or political subdivisions were covered if they used any test or device as a condition for voter registration on November 1, 1964, and either less than 50% of voting age persons living there were registered to vote on that date or less than 50% voted in the presidential election that year. The definition of a "test or device" included any prerequisite for registration or voting to demonstrate a person's literacy, educational achievement or knowledge of any particular subject, good moral character, or prove his or her qualifications by the voucher of registered voters or others. The jurisdictions that were covered by Section 4(b) in 1965 were Alabama, Georgia, Louisiana, Mississippi, South Carolina, Virginia, 39 counties in North Carolina, and specified counties in Arizona and Hawaii. The coverage formula provision was intended to be temporary, but was reauthorized in 1970, 1975, 1982, and 2006, when it was extended until 2031.

As the VRA was amended and new provisions were added, other states and political subdivisions were added under the coverage formula, adjusted according to the presidential election year in which a test or device had been used as a condition of registration or voting (1968, and 1972). The 1972 amendments added the "minority language provision" that included under the coverage formula those jurisdictions where voting information was provided only in English and members of a single language minority were more than 5% of the citizens of voting age (see section below on 1972 amendments). As discussed in the "Concluding Observations" section of this report and elsewhere, the coverage formula was found unconstitutional by the U.S. Supreme Court in June 2013.

Preclearance of Changes to Election Laws (Sec. 5)

Section 5 is inoperable currently due to the U.S. Supreme Court decision in *Shelby County v. Holder*, which found that Section 4(b) of the VRA unconstitutional (see the discussion of the case in the "Summary" and "Concluding Observations" sections of this report). As originally enacted, Section 5 prevents states and political subdivisions covered under Section 4 from enacting any new voting "qualification or prerequisite to voting, or standard, practice, or procedure with respect to voting different from that in force or effect on November 1, 1964."[73] As such, it "freezes" voting procedures already in place and requires covered jurisdictions to submit any changes to the voting process for review—called "preclearance"—by the U.S. Department of

---

[70] The speech made be found at http://www.justice.gov/iso/opa/ag/speeches/2013/ag-speech-130725 html .

[71] For a detailed discussion of the coverage formula, see CRS Legal Sidebar, The Voting Rights Act: How Does the Coverage Formula Work? How Does a Covered Jurisdiction Get Released from Coverage?, by L. Paige Whitaker

[72] 42 U.S.C. §1973b.

[73] 42 U.S.C. §1973c.

Justice or the U.S. District Court for the District of Columbia (in an action for a declaratory judgment) to determine if the change would have a discriminatory purpose or effect. Section 5 was designed to prevent states and political subdivisions from circumventing the goal of expanded black registration and voting by simply enacting new disenfranchisement practices and procedures, as had been done throughout the 20th century. The number of covered jurisdictions subject to the preclearance requirement expanded over time to include many outside the South, with a freeze date to reflect when coverage began. Until the Supreme Court's decision in *Shelby County*, nine states were wholly covered (Alabama, Alaska, Arizona, Georgia, Louisiana, Mississippi, South Carolina, Texas, and Virginia) and six more were covered in part (California, Florida, Michigan, New York, North Carolina, and South Dakota).[74]

Changes to the voting process that are subject to preclearance may have neither the purpose nor the effect of discriminating against minority voters. Therefore, the Attorney General or the U.S. District Court for the District of Columbia can block implementation of a law that is not intended to be discriminatory if it is determined that it would result in denying or abridging minority voting rights. Whether the Attorney General or the court conducts the review, "[t]he burden of establishing that a proposed voting change is nondiscriminatory falls on the jurisdiction."[75] In cases where a proposed change is submitted to the Attorney General for review—called administrative review—the change may go into effect if the Attorney General "affirmatively indicates no objection" or does not notify the jurisdiction of an objection within 60 days of submission. Most voting changes are submitted for review to the Attorney General, who has received 14,000 to 24,000 submissions of voting changes per year during the past decade.[76] Judicial review of a proposed change by a three judge panel of the U.S. District Court for the District of Columbia may take longer than administrative review and an appeal of a decision goes directly to the U.S. Supreme Court. The defendant in such cases is the United States or the Attorney General.

Section 5 has been subject to various legal challenges, beginning in 1966 when it was upheld by the U.S. Supreme Court in *South Carolina v. Katzenbach*.[77] South Carolina challenged the constitutionality of the Section 5 preclearance provision, which the Court determined was a valid exercise of congressional powers under Section 2 of the Fifteenth Amendment. After Section 5 was reauthorized in 1975, the Court reaffirmed the *Katzenbach* ruling in *City of Rome v. United States*[78] and again in *Lopez v. Monterey County*[79] after its 1985 reauthorization. In a 2009 challenge (following the 2006 reauthorization), the Court ruled that a utility district in Texas was eligible to be released from coverage, but did not rule on the constitutionality of Section 5 in the case, *Northwest Austin Municipal Utility District Number One (NAMUDNO) v. Holder*.[80] However, the court observed that Section 5 raises "serious constitutional questions."[81]

---

[74] For a list of covered states and jurisdictions, see the U.S. Department of Justice website at http://www.justice.gov/crt/about/vot/sec_5/covered.php.

[75] U.S. Department of Justice website at http://www.justice.gov/crt/about/vot/sec_5/about.php.

[76] A chronological listing of objections may be found at http://www.justice.gov/crt/about/vot/sec_5/obj_activ.php.

[77] 383 U.S. 301.

[78] 446 U.S. 156, 183 (1980).

[79] 525 U.S. 266 (1999).

[80] 129 S.Ct. 2504 (2009).

[81] For a detailed discussion of Court rulings on Section 5, see CRS Report R42482, *Congressional Redistricting and the Voting Rights Act: A Legal Overview*, by L. Paige Whitaker.

Release From Coverage or "Bailout" (Sec. 4(a))

States and political jurisdictions that were subject to the coverage formula under Section 4(b) before *Shelby County v. Holder* and the corresponding preclearance requirement under Section 5 could seek to be released from coverage under a process known as "bailout." A state or jurisdiction could seek a declaratory judgment from a three judge panel in the U.S. District Court for the District of Columbia by demonstrating that, during the previous 10 years, no discriminatory test or device has been used, the state or jurisdiction has complied with preclearance requirements, no adverse legal judgments or pending lawsuits concerning voting discrimination exist, and there have been no violations of federal, state, or local voting discrimination laws (other than trivial violations that were immediately corrected). Furthermore, practices that result in vote dilution or inhibit equal access to voting must have been eliminated, intimidation and harassment of persons seeking to participate in the voting process has been eliminated, and minority participation in voting and the presence of appointed minority officials at all levels of the electoral process must be evident. The criteria apply to all units of government in the jurisdiction, including cities, towns, school districts, and other entities.[82]

A list of states in which some jurisdictions within the state have bailed out of VRA coverage since 1967 includes Alabama, California, Colorado, Connecticut, Georgia, Hawaii, Idaho, Massachusetts, New Hampshire, New Mexico, North Carolina, Oklahoma, Texas, Virginia, and Wyoming.[83] No state has bailed out of coverage.

Prohibition of Literacy Requirement for Citizens Educated in American-flag Schools (Section 4(e))

Section 4(e) provides that persons with limited English proficiency cannot be denied the right to register and vote. Specifically, it states that those who have completed sixth grade "in a public school, or a private school accredited by any state, territory, the District of Columbia, or the Commonwealth of Puerto Rico" cannot be denied the right to vote because of "an inability to read, write, understand, or interpret any matter in the English language."[84] In a state where state law provides for a different level of education to presume literacy, the equivalent level of education in a public school or accredited private in which the predominant classroom language was other than English shall be demonstrated. The provision concerned the large number of Puerto Ricans in New York City at the time that had been educated in "American-flag schools [in Puerto Rico] in which the predominant classroom language was other than English."[85] Between 1950 and 1963, an average of 50,000 Puerto Ricans migrated to New York City each year.[86]

---

[82] A detailed description of the bailout criteria may be found on the Department of Justice website at http://www.justice.gov/crt/about/vot/misc/sec_4.php.

[83] Ibid.

[84] 42 U.S.C. §1973b(e).

[85] Ibid.

[86] "The Puerto Rican Community: Its Political Background," in *Latinos and the Political System*, ed. F. Chris Garcia (Notre Dame, IN: University of Notre Dame Press, 1988), p. 65.

Appointment of Federal Examiners for Voter Registration (Sections 6 and 7) and of Federal Election Observers (Section 8)

To facilitate voter registration, the Attorney General is authorized to request the appointment of federal examiners in covered jurisdictions whenever 20 or more residents of a political subdivision have submitted written complaints that they have been denied the right to vote on account of race or color, or whenever such appointment is deemed necessary in the judgment of the Attorney General (Section 6). The names of applicants who are determined to be eligible to vote are placed on the voter registration list by the examiners (Section 7).

Section 8 authorizes the appointment of election observers in any political subdivision where an examiner has been assigned to observe "whether persons who are entitled to vote are being permitted to vote" and whether their votes are being properly tabulated.

Amendments

The VRA has been reauthorized and amended five times since it was enacted in 1965, in 1970, 1975, 1982, 1992, and 2006. The amendments are summarized below.

1970

Set to expire on August 6, 1970, the VRA of 1965 was extended for five years when it was amended and signed it into law by President Richard M. Nixon on June 22, 1970.[87] In addition, the 1970 amendments to the law extended from 5 to 10 years the prohibition on using literacy tests and similar devices in jurisdictions covered under Section 4(b).

H.R. 4249, the "Voting Rights Act Amendments of 1970," was passed in the House on December 11, 1969[88] and referred to the Senate, where an amended version was passed on March 13, 1970, on a 64-12 roll call vote.[89] The House agreed to the Senate amendments to H.R. 4249 when it approved the bill on a roll call vote of 272-132 on June 17, 1970.[90]

In addition to the provisions noted above, others required the following:

- that durational residency requirements be abolished in presidential elections and directed each state to provide for the registration and qualification of all duly qualified residents who apply to vote not later than 30 days before an election and permit those who moved to a jurisdiction within 30 days of an election to vote in person in the place of their previous residence or by absentee ballot, if eligible to do so;

---

[87] P.L. 91-285.

[88] "Extension of Voting Rights Act of 1965," House debate, *Congressional Record*, vol. 115, part 28 (December 11, 1969), pp. 38536-38537.

[89] "Voting Rights Act Amendments of 1969," Remarks in the Senate, *Congressional Record*, vol. 116, part 6 (March 13, 1970), p. 7336.

[90] "Extending Voting Rights Act of 1965," House debate, *Congressional Record*, vol. 116, part 15 (June 17, 1970), pp. 20199-20200.

- that the ban on the use of literacy tests and similar devices be extended to all states until August 6, 1975;

- that the coverage formula apply to all states and counties in which a literacy test was used and less than 50% of voting age residents were registered or voted in the 1968 presidential election, thereby including parts of Alaska, Arizona, California, Idaho, New York, and Oregon;[91]

- that the voting age be lowered to 18;[92]

1975

The VRA came up for renewal again in 1975, when President Gerald R. Ford signed a seven-year extension on August 6, 1975.[93]

H.R. 6219 was passed in the House on June 4, 1975, on a 341-70 vote.[94] The Senate passed an amended version of the bill on a 77-12 vote on July 24;[95] the House agreed to the Senate amendments on a 346-56 vote on July 28.[96]

In addition to extending the law for seven years, other provisions did the following:

- extended the coverage formula, or "trigger," that required preclearance of voting changes for an additional seven years, meaning that states or political jurisdictions that were covered in 1965 could not be released from coverage until 1982 if there was a discriminatory test or device in place during the previous 17 years and those covered in 1970 could not be released until 1987;

- extended for seven years the method under which covered states and political jurisdictions could "bail out" of coverage, which entailed obtaining a judgment from the U.S. District Court for the District of Columbia that the jurisdiction had not used a discriminatory test or device since 1964;

- made permanent the temporary ban on the use of literacy tests for voter registration nationally and extended it as well to jurisdictions already subject to the coverage formula so that such tests could not be reinstituted if the jurisdiction was released from coverage;

- expanded the protections of Section 5 preclearance and Section 8 federal observers to jurisdictions in which 5% of voting age citizens were from a single language minority, election materials were printed only in English, and less than

---

[91] *Congressional Quarterly Almanac, 1970*, (Washington: Congressional Quarterly, 1971), p. 192.

[92] In Oregon v. Mitchell, 400 U.S. 112 (1970), the U.S. Supreme Court ruled that Congress could set the age requirement for federal elections, but it could not set an age requirement for state and local elections. The twenty-sixth amendment, ratified in 1971, set the voting age for all elections at 18.

[93] P.L. 94-73.

[94] "Voting Rights Act Extension," House debate, *Congressional Record*, vol. 121, part 13 (June 4, 1975), pp. 16916-16917.

[95] "Amendment of the Voting Rights Act," Remarks in the Senate, *Congressional Record*, vol. 121, part 19 (July 24, 1975), p. 24780.

[96] "Provide for Consideration of H.R. 6219, Amending the Voting Rights Act of 1965," House debate, *Congressional Record*, vol. 121, part 20 (July 28, 1975), p. 25220.

50% of voting age citizens were registered for or voted in the 1972 presidential election (and included a bail out provision if English only elections had not been a barrier in the previous 10 years);

- added a requirement for bilingual elections (but did not authorize Section 5 preclearance and Section 8 federal observers) if the Census Bureau determined that 5% of voting age citizens in a jurisdiction were from a single language minority and the illiteracy rate in English was greater than the national illiteracy in English (and included a provision to allow a jurisdiction to discontinue bilingual elections when it could demonstrate in a federal court that the illiteracy rate of the language minority had dropped below the national illiteracy rate);

- authorized individuals (in addition to the DOJ) to bring suit to impose a preclearance requirement and the use of federal examiners in a jurisdiction;

- required the U.S. Census Bureau to conduct surveys in covered jurisdictions after every election for the U.S. House of Representatives, beginning in 1974, to collect registration and voting statistics by age, race, and national origin (but stipulated that no person could be compelled to disclose any information, including race, national origin, voting status, etc., sought by the Bureau in the survey);

- directed the Attorney General to take action against states and jurisdictions to require implementation of the 26th Amendment that set the voting age at 18 and established a penalty of up to $5,000 or five years imprisonment for anyone who would deny or attempt to deny the anyone eligible under the amendment;

- established a penalty of up to $10,000 or five years imprisonment for voting more than once in a federal election.

1982

President Ronald W. Reagan signed a renewal of the VRA on June 29, 1982, that extended for 25 years the Section 5 preclearance provision, which was set to expire on August 6, 1982, and extended the requirement for bilingual elections for 10 years.[97]

H.R. 3112 was passed in the House on October 5, 1981, on a 389-24 vote.[98] It was subsequently passed in the Senate, with amendments, on June 18, 1982, on a 85-8 vote,[99] following a filibuster by opponents. The House approved the Senate-amended version by unanimous consent on October 5.[100]

Other provisions of the law did the following:

---

[97] P.L. 97-205.

[98] "Voting Rights Act Extension," House debate, *Congressional Record*, vol. 127, part 17 (October 5, 1981), p. 23205.

[99] "Voting Rights Act Amendments of 1982," Remarks in the Senate, *Congressional Record*, vol. 128, part 11 (June 18, 1982), p. 14337.

[100] "Voting Rights Act of 1965 Amendments," House debate, *Congressional Record*, vol. 128, part 11 (June 23, 1982), p. 14940.

- extended by two years, until 1984, the period of time in which states and jurisdictions covered under the preclearance provision could seek release from coverage, meaning that a jurisdiction could not have used a discriminatory test or device as a condition for voter registration for the previous 19, rather than 17 years;

- amended Section 2 to provide that a voting rights violation could be established under the section by showing that it had resulted in discrimination, a change intended to address the finding in *Mobile v. Bolden*[101] that an intent to discriminate was necessary to constitute a violation;

- permitted a political subdivision of a covered state to seek to be released from coverage separately from the state.

1992

President George H.W. Bush signed an extension of the VRA on August 26, 1992, which amended two provisions that concerned bilingual voting assistance (discussed in greater detail below).

H.R. 4312 was passed in the House on June 24, 1992, on a 237-125 vote.[102] It was passed in the Senate on August 7, 1992, on a 75-20 vote.[103]

The law's provisions

- extended the requirement for bilingual voting assistance for an additional 15 years, until 2007;

- expanded the scope of coverage for bilingual voting assistance to include jurisdictions with 10,000 members of a language minority whose members have limited English proficiency

2006

President George W. Bush signed a reauthorization of the VRA on July 27, 2006;[104] it was due to come up for renewal in 2007.

The House passed H.R. 9 on July 13, 2006, on a 390-33 vote.[105] The Senate passed the bill on July 20 on a 98-0 vote.[106]

---

[101] 446 U.S. 55 (1980).

[102] "Voting Rights Language Assistance Act of 1992," House debate, *Congressional Record*, vol. 138, part 14 (July 24, 1992), pp. 19344-19345.

[103] "Voting Rights Language Assistance Act," remarks in the Senate, *Congressional Record*, vol. 138, part 16 (August 7, 1992), p. 22198.

[104] P.L. 109-246

[105] "Fannie Lou Hamer, Rosa Parks, and Coretta Scott King Voting Rights Act Reauthorization and Amendments Act of 2006," House debate, *Congressional Record*, daily edition, vol. 152 (July 13, 2006), p. H5207.

[106] "Fannie Lou Hamer, Rosa Parks, and Coretta Scott King Voting Rights Act Reauthorization and Amendments Act of 2006," remarks in the Senate, *Congressional Record*, daily edition, vol. 152 (July 20, 2006), p. S8012.

The law's provisions

- included a statement of findings that cited, for example, a continued need for the law, based on evidence of discrimination against minority voters and the reduced effectiveness of the law due to U.S. Supreme Court decisions "which have misconstrued Congress' original intent in enacting the Voting Rights Act of 1965," and "evidence before Congress [that] reveals that 40 years has not been a sufficient amount of time to eliminate the vestiges of discrimination following nearly 100 years of disregard for the dictates of the Fifteenth Amendment";[107]

- extended the law for 25 years, until 2032;

- eliminated the role of federal election examiners to register voters, but retained the possible use of election observers in polling places by the Department of Justice;

- authorized payment for expert witnesses to parties who won lawsuits under the law;

- extended the bilingual voting assistance provision for 25 years, until 2032;

- directed that American Community Survey census data be used to determine where bilingual voting assistance was needed, rather than long-form census data from the decennial census.

Legislation Overview

113th Congress

Two identical bills, H.R. 3399 and S. 1945, have been introduced that would amend the VRA to include a new formula to replace the Section 4(b) coverage formula that the U.S. Supreme Court found unconstitutional in June 2013. The bills would require preclearance of changes to the voting process by the state (and all of its political subdivisions) if, during the previous 15 years, five or more voting rights violations occurred in the state, at least 1 of which was committed by the state itself, rather than by a subdivision. Coverage would apply to specific political subdivisions in which three or more violations had occurred in the previous 15 years, or one violation had occurred in the previous 15 years and minority turnout had been extremely low during that period. According to the legislation, a violation would occur in a state or political subdivision if, in a final judgment,

- any court determined that a denial or abridgement of the right to vote on account of race, color, or membership in a language minority in violation of the Fourteenth or Fifteenth Amendments; or

- any court determined that a voting qualification or standard, practice, or procedure was imposed "in a manner that resulted or would have resulted in the denial or abridgement of the right to vote based on race or color, or in

---

[107] §2.

contravention of the guarantees of set forth in subsection (f)(2), in violation of Section 2" of the VRA;[108] or

- any court denied a request for a declaratory judgment under Section 3(c) or 5 of the VRA; or

- the Attorney General interposed an objection under Section 3(c) or 5, other than an objection to a voting qualification requiring photo identification

In addition, the bills would amend Section 3(c) to expand the types of violations that trigger a court to retain jurisdiction in a state or political subdivision—also known as the "bail in" provision (discussed on page 15 of this report). Currently, violations of the 14th or 15th Amendments may result in a court retaining jurisdiction, during which time no electoral change may be made without court approval. As amended by the legislation, additional triggering violations would include the Voting Rights Act (other than a violation of Section 2(a) that is based on the requirement that an individual provide photo identification to vote) and any federal voting rights law that prohibits discrimination on the basis of race, color, or membership in a language minority group.

States or political subdivisions would be required to provide public notice in the state or political subdivision and on the Internet of changes in prerequisites, standards, practices, or procedures that are different from what was in effect 180 days before the election. The public notice would have to be provided no later than 48 hours after making the change.

The bills would clarify that the Attorney General could assign observers to enforce the Fourteenth and Fifteenth Amendments, the VRA, and any other law to protect voting rights, including assigning observers to enforce bilingual election requirements. Finally, the requirements for injunctive relief would be revised; the scope would be expanded to include the Fourteenth and Fifteenth Amendments, the VRA, and any federal voting rights law that prohibits discrimination on the basis of race, color, or membership in a language minority group; and the persons authorized to seek relief would be expanded to include an aggrieved person, in addition to the Attorney General.

The standard under which a court would grant relief would change if either bill was enacted. The bills would require a court to grant relief if it determined that, on balance, the hardship imposed on the defendant would be less than the hardship imposed on the plaintiff if relief were not granted. The court would be required to consider several factors, including

- the qualification, prerequisite, standard, practice, or procedure in effect prior to when the change was adopted as a remedy for a federal court judgment; consent decree or admission; or served as a ground for dismissal or settlement of a claim regarding discrimination based on race or color in violation of the 14th or 15th Amendment; a violation of the VRA; or voting discrimination based on race, color, or membership in a language minority group, in violation of any other federal or state law;

[108] 2 U.S.C. §1973b(f)(2) provides: "No voting qualification or prerequisite to voting, or standard, practice, or procedure shall be imposed or applied by any State or political subdivision to deny or abridge the right of any citizen of the United States to vote because he is a member of a language minority group."

- the change was adopted less than 180 days prior to the election and the defendant failed to provide adequate notice of the change as required under federal or state law.

Concluding Observations

The *Shelby County* case concerned a challenge to the Section 5 preclearance provision in the law, specifically whether Congress exceeded its authority when it reauthorized Section 5—and the related coverage formula in Section 4—for another 25 years in 2006, thereby violating the Constitution. The Court noted that, because Congress failed to update the coverage formula following its ruling in *Northwest Austin Municipal Utility District Number One v. Holder* [109] (see discussion on page 17 of this report), it left the Court "no choice but to declare §4(b) unconstitutional. The formula in that section can no longer be used as a basis for subjecting jurisdictions to preclearance."[110] The Court did not issue an opinion on Section 5. Consequently, the Section 5 preclearance requirement is suspended in the absence of a coverage formula that determines which states or political subdivisions are subject to the requirement.

Even prior to last year's U.S. Supreme Court ruling, some observers had suggested that the Section 5 pre-clearance provision was anachronistic and no longer necessary because racial dynamics had changed since the 1960s. They argued that the remedial purpose of Section 5, based on racial voting patterns in the 1960s, had become a burden to covered jurisdictions.[111] Other provisions of the law had drawn criticism as well, such as the requirement to provide voting materials in languages other than English in jurisdictions with a concentrated language minority or minorities.[112]

In anticipation of the *Shelby County* decision, the NAACP had noted that " ... the loss of Section 5 would mean that voters of color and our allies would need to rely upon case-by-case litigation under Section 2 of the Voting Rights Act, as well as whatever protections may be available under various state laws and state constitutions, to safeguard rights of all voters."[113] Although the Court did not rule on the constitutionality of Section 5, it is inoperable unless or until a new coverage formula is enacted. The organization also suggested that Section 2 challenges would likely be less effective, at least initially: "The reason why Section 2 is much less effective than Section 5, however, is that Section 5 blocks discriminatory laws *before* they take effect and, therefore, *before* they can illegally harm minority voters."[114]

Although the VRA had not been an active legislative area for Congress since the law was last reauthorized in 2006, the Supreme Court ruling will shape the future of debate about the VRA and determine where that debate occurs, either in Congress, or the courts, or both. In any case, because of the prominence of the VRA for the past 50 years, voting rights policy in the aftermath

---

[109] 129 S.Ct. 2504 (2009).

[110] 133 S. Ct. 2612 (2013) at 2631.

[111] Ilya Shapiro, "Discrimination is Now Discrete, Not Pandemic," *The New York Times*, February 24, 2013, at http://www.nytimes.com/roomfordebate/2013/02/24/is-the-voting-rights-act-still-needed/discrimination-is-now-discrete-not-pandemic.

[112] Linda Chavez, "Bilingual ballots are a costly, bad idea," *Grand Rapids Press*, August 21, p. A14.

[113] From NAACP website http://www.naacpldf.org/files/case_issue/Shelby-County-Alabama-v-Holder-Q&A.pdf.

[114] Ibid.

---

of the Supreme Court decision is somewhat unpredictable and could be the focus of sustained Congressional interest for some time.

Author Contact Information

Kevin J. Coleman
Analyst in Elections
kcoleman@crs.loc.gov, 7-7878